springboard
TO SUCCESS

Strategies To Keep Business Casual
From Making Business…Casual

April Callis

Kensington Press

Springboard to Success:
Strategies To Keep Business Casual From Making
Business...Casual

Printed in the United States of America

Library of Congress Cataloging-in-Publication Data

Callis, April L.
        Springboard to Success: Strategies To Keep
        Business Casual From Making Business...Casual

Library of Congress Cataloging Number: 2005924588

ISBN 0-9765171-0-8

Cover Design by Bryce Erwin

Published by
Kensington Press
403 Kensington Road
East Lansing, Michigan 48823

Contents

Acknowledgements

There are many people to acknowledge, all of whom were supportive and encouraging, and many of who contributed their valuable insights and expertise to the writing of this book.

It is appropriate to start with Pat Materka for her belief, enthusiasm, and amazing editorial skills. Jennifer Bayse Sander, for her encouragement and reminders of persistence and Peg Lutz, for providing focus and an extra hand where needed.

Thanks to Lisa Pascoe, for listening supportively and offering suggestions as only a true friend can and Jene Janich for her friendship and reminders about the importance of this topic. Many thanks to NSA-Michigan for friendship and support, especially to Renee Merchant, Karen Bell-Brege and Joanne Estes for believing in me.

I must also thank my parents, John and Carol for their faith and unwavering belief in me, as well as my husband Andy, for his love and understanding. Last, but certainly not least I want to thank my beautiful daughters, whose patience with this project has been both remarkable and humbling. To my darling flower girls, Violet May, Emma Rose and Lily Grace, thank you for your belief and love.

Introduction

Business causal began with a great impulse.
In the late 1980's and early 1990's, a number of
organizations began to move to a business casual
dress code. As a consultant for Ford Motor
Company during this period, I was able to witness
this transformation first hand. In order to create
more of a team environment, the company
decided that managers should stop wearing
traditional business suits and ties and dress
more informally to better relate with their non-
exempt and union co-workers. The belief was
that eliminating differences in appearance
between various levels of employees would
increase cohesiveness and make the workplace
more productive. This meant that many
administrative-level employees who had
previously only worn suits, now had to replace

their entire wardrobes with clothing that was considered business-like and yet – "casual."

Although part of the intent of business casual was to erase the lines between the managers and the rest of the staff, the "casual" clothing that the managers began wearing redrew the line. Hand knit sweaters from Australia that cost between $350 and $1,000 dollars quickly replaced the suit jacket and tie.

And while the managers were busy establishing new standards of status, midlevel staff struggled with the definition of this new term. Is a short-sleeved dress shirt business casual?

How about a polo shirt, if it has a collar? If khaki's are business casual, then are jeans ever acceptable?

While business casual may have started as a dress code, it has become more than that. It has become a way of doing business, a new culture. In fact for employees who have entered the workforce during the last decade, it is the only type of environment they have known. The rules are unwritten and subtle.

This book will guide you in presenting yourself professionally, even in a business casual workplace. Because presenting a professional image is not about wardrobe, it's how you communicate, listen, follow through, and conduct yourself in a variety of situations. And yes, it is how you appear to others as well.

As business casual attire has become commonplace, the work environment has changed. Behavior has become more relaxed as well. As a result, organizations and individuals are not as effective as they could be, and many employees are left wondering how to be perceived as promotion worthy and professional.

Business casual has in fact made business... casual. The purpose of this book is to help you discover how to present a professional image and conduct yourself with professional manner that transcends appearances.

1

Presenting a Professional Image

Presenting a Professional Image

The way you look, speak, dress, walk and interact communicates information about you to others and contributes to the impressions others have of you. These attributes in the context of your work are your "Professional Image".

You may be concerned about your image right now for a couple of reasons. Perhaps someone has recommended that you focus more carefully on how you present yourself. Maybe you feel there is something blocking you and your career, and you are not where you want to be. Or possibly you believe you have been displaying your skills, and ability, and have been waiting patiently to be promoted – yet you've been repeatedly passed over. What, you wonder, is holding you back?

We will cover a lot of information in this book about elements that affect one's professional image. I will give you new tools to use to present yourself in the most favorable light. Whatever the stage of your career, feel free to apply as much or as little as seems relevant to your personal needs. My hope for you is that you can become a treasure hunter and apply the golden nuggets of information to your own situation to better meet your goals.

We will examine:
- What is a professional image?

- How to make a great first impression
- How to use your nonverbal skills to enhance your message
- Proper business attire for today's work environment
- Why proper business etiquette still matters
- How polishing your presentation skills can boost your image

And finally, we'll discuss techniques for presenting yourself in the best light in a job interview, because the entire objective of this book is to move you ahead. Let the chapters that follow be your *Springboard for Success.*

2

Your Professional Image

What is a professional image?

Your professional image is two sides of a mirror, it is how you see yourself, and it's the impression you make on others.

Your professional image is an expression of your identity that conveys your self-esteem and self-worth. Essentially, it's the kind of person you consider yourself to be, what you want others to feel about you.

It is important to be aware of this image and what it is you are presenting. It's not trite or superficial, because people make judgments, and are constantly forming perceptions about others based upon what they see and hear. You may say, "well, that's not right; it's not fair," but it's a reality. Perception and judgment is the way people make sense of the world.

Your professional image is composed of a number of elements. What you say, what you wear, how you act, how you are heard, and how you listen all contribute to the impression you make on those around you. It is important to understand the message you're sending, so that you can be sure you are conveying the image you want.

Why should I care?

You should care about your professional image, because it can hold you back or speed you ahead in your career and other aspects of your personal life. It can be a reason that you are – or are not – the person who comes to mind when your supervisor or coworkers are assessing potential. You can have all the talents and training that you need, but if your image is out of sync with your credentials, you will not go forward. Your professional image must match who you are and who you *want to be.*

Perception

Humans use perception to organize and understand the world around them. Our perceptions help us quickly familiarize ourselves with new things or situations, based on what we already know. We build on prior knowledge to understand new information. Without our perceptions, we'd have to figure out everything over and over again. For example, without perception we couldn't even get out of the house because we would look at a doorknob and think, "what is this for?" Then, we would turn it and pull it and discover that the door opens. And then we'd get to our car and have to figure that out.

We use our perceptions as a short cut to make our lives easier, relating unknown things to known things. Using these short cuts can also be somewhat misleading and risky because sometimes we jump to the wrong conclusions. Perception consists of Recognition, Interpretation and Expectation.

Recognition

Recognition is the process of comparing something new with what we already know to see what is familiar about the new process, person or situation. When we encounter something new, our brain searches our own mental database and asks, "What does this look like?" For example, though I may not have been in a particular building before, I **recognize** that the door opens, the lobby has elevator banks and the buttons on the wall will signal an elevator to open at the lobby. Recognition is a perceptual shortcut to ensure that we don't have to learn everything over and over again.

Interpretation

Interpretation helps us figure out what we are recognizing. Interpretation is the meaning that we assign to what we recognize. When we encounter something new, we shift through our past experiences. Once we recognize what is happening, we interpret what it means. To continue our example, my **interpretation** of the elevator buttons in the lobby is that there is more than one floor to this building and if I want to reach a different floor quickly, then I should use the elevator. Interpretation helps us figure out what we're recognizing.

Expectation

Based on our own recognition and interpretation, we create expectation. Expectation is very powerful. Experience influences our expectations in each unique situation. For example, when I press the elevator button, my expectation is that the elevator doors will open and I will step in to the elevator and select the floor I'd like by pushing another button. When this occurs my **expectation** is fulfilled and my perception is reinforced. The theory of self-fulfilling prophecy (the idea that what is expected to happen does happen because we tend to fulfill our own expectations) is based on the power of expectation.

We can use the power of perceptions to our advantage. John, a communications professor, relied on the power of perception to help him survive his first teaching experience:

"The first time I ever had to teach a college class, I was terrified. I had taught training seminars and given many presentations, but I was nervous about teaching my first real class at an urban community college. Most of the students were non-traditional, so many of them were my own age or older. I had my textbook and my notes and sat behind the desk waiting for the students to arrive. So, there I was facing my first class and not sure how to get the class started. So I asked myself, "what

would a teacher do?" A teacher would tell them to open their books. So I said, "Hello everyone, please open your books to page 4. " And they did! I was so excited and it was a great revelation to me that they recognized me behind the desk as their teacher. Their interpretation was that they should do what the teacher told them if they wanted to be successful in the class, and then they formed an expectation based on their recognition and interpretation, which I fulfilled by asking them to open their books and behaving like a teacher."

Cognitive Dissonance

Another element of perception can be cognitive dissonance. Cognitive dissonance is when what you expect to happen is so different from what does happen that it gives you a sense of being off balance and out of control. When what we expect to happen does not happen, or when an expectation we have is fulfilled in a way that is far different from what we expect, it creates a sense of dissonance -- a feeling that something is very wrong.

During the attacks of September 11th Americans experienced a collective sense of cognitive dissonance. What was happening was so far outside of our expectations, we could hardly recognize the situation, and there was no historical background to interpret it. The entire U.S. population was reeling from the sense of cognitive dissonance that was created.

Back to our teaching example: If John had just sat and stared at the class participants for an hour, he would not have met their expectations. Or, if he had begun crying, or fled from the room, he would have created cognitive dissonance. Expectation is a powerful force.

> *"The students expected me to teach them something," John said. "They didn't know that they were my first class they perceived me as their teacher. Their expectations were met."*

What image are you projecting?

Perception is reality. As human beings, we use our recognition, interpretation and expectations to form our perceptions and what we believe is real. We may not recognize how others perceive us. Participants in my professional image seminars often complain, "People think that I am ineffective and I don't know why" or "I'm doing something that's sending the wrong message, and I'm not really clear on what I'm doing."

At a corporate seminar on interviewing skills, I met Susan, a short, pretty brunette in her early thirties. Her long brown hair was pulled back with a headband, and she wore a pink fluffy sweater and long black skirt with boots. I assumed that she was an administrative assistant or in human resources. Her petite size, choice of clothing and long girlish hair gave her a very vulnerable and feminine appearance. During the mock interview session she confided that she was taking the class because she had been on a number of unsuccessful interviews. Although she was well qualified for the positions that she was seeking, she had not received a single job offer. She had even been passed over for promotion. This woman had an MBA and an engineering degree, yet her appearance suggested she was barely out of college.

Let's take a look at some pictures, and you decide what type of business these individuals work in, what type of position they hold, and what kind of car they drive. Remember, the way we are perceived by others is in reality who we are to them.

What if I tell you that this woman is an attorney? If that surprises you, you are not alone. In my classes most people guess that she is a social worker, customer service representative or Girl Scout leader. They also guess that the car she drives is a Ford Focus, Taurus, or some other small American- made car. (She actually drives a Lexus). Who she is and where she works does not match the way that she presents herself. She doesn't look like anyone's image of an attorney! When you have a mismatch or disconnect, that's when you have a serious image problem. Would you go to her if you needed legal help? This image is not good for her business.

Let's look at another one:

Hostess, entertainer, hairdresser, model, dancer – this is what my classes usually guess and they are right.

This is a picture of an actress/model. She is dressed glamorously. The way that she presents herself matches who she is, and the sexy star image that she wants to convey.

Here's another one. Is he a college kid? Pizza delivery guy? Unemployed?

He is an insurance agent. He doesn't convey trust and security though does he. When who you are and what you do does not match your career may suffer as a result.

Ok, the last one.
My classes generally guess lawyer, doctor or CEO.

The first answer is right. This man is a partner in a law firm — in fact, the same firm that the first woman we looked at works for. So if you need an attorney, who are you going to choose – the Girl Scout leader, or this guy? I would choose him because if I'm going to spend money for an attorney I want one who looks like an attorney! His appearance inspires confidence.

Sometimes an image mismatch can be good. One of my college professors was consistently mistaken for the janitor. He was one of the smartest and most talented educators that I've ever met and yet people were always asking him to take out the trash. He walked around with big keys on his belt, wearing a flannel shirt. He knew this was the image he was projecting and used it to his advantage to observe students when they were not on their best behavior and to avoid administrators who were looking for a faculty member to give prospective parents a tour. Because he was the technical director of the theatre and built sets for the plays on a daily basis his "uniform" was practical as well. It was a good match for him.

If who you are and what you are presenting do not match, that's when you have a problem.

3

First Impressions

First Impressions

Keeping in mind that what we perceive as real is real, you can see the importance of how you present yourself initially - your first impression.

Let's say you are starting a new job at my office. Your first day on the job, I initially perceive you to be very professional. You arrive looking great, carrying a brief case; you shake my hand and carry yourself with confidence. Then you say, "oh, gawd, I can't stand coming in on a day that it's this nice. What the hell are we here for...?"

This mismatch in your appearance and behavior causes me cognitive dissonance. What you said and how you said it throws me completely. My first visual impression was positive, but it has been contradicted and reformed by your comments.

Remember that there are a number of things that contribute to your first impression: your clothing, appearance, words and posture. In the chapters ahead, we'll discuss aspects of all of them.

Six Ways to Ensure a Great First Impression

1. Smile!

First and foremost, smile. When you smile at people, you are opening the door to communication with them, and they will perceive you as an open and friendly person. If you smile too much, you can be perceived as nervous, so a nice smile, just long enough to make it through "nice to meet you" will do. Women are more likely to smile than men, but people of every age and gender appreciate the gesture. If you want to make a great first impression flash those teeth!

2. Eye Contact

Look people in the eye. Good eye contact is key to a good impression. If this makes you uncomfortable, try looking at one eye. Do not try to look at the forehead or eyebrows; people can tell if you are not looking them in the eye. They cannot, however, tell the difference between looking at one eye or both eyes. Television and film actors use the one eye technique for close up work, as looking at both eyes of another person can cause your eyes to shift back and forth slightly – giving you a "shifty eyed" look.

Eye contact is personal; if you are looking at someone and they stop looking at you, it may be because your eye contact feels intrusive. One of the benefits of good eye contact is that it enables you to monitor nonverbal behavior. I've encountered many people who believe they are giving good eye contact but are actually looking at the ceiling tiles or the floor while speaking or listening.

I had the opportunity to see President Bill Clinton give a speech in person at one time. He was an eye contact master. He met the eyes of each individual audience member in front of him (mostly college faculty and staff), and then I watched him look into the bleachers on both sides of the gym to make eye contact with the students. Each of us in the audience came away feeling as though we had just had a personal conversation with him, just because of the genuine and powerful eye contact.

3. Posture

Good posture gives you the appearance of energy and confidence. Picture the difference between standing straight and tall, or slouched and round-shouldered. Good posture does not mean that you look like you are standing at attention like a military officer, but your shoulders should be back and your head held high. One way to achieve good posture is to imagine that you have a string connected to the crown of your head that is pulling you upward. Practice good posture until it becomes second nature. I usually practice when I'm waiting in lines at the bank or supermarket, or preparing a meal. Find a time to practice and make it a habit.

4. Movement

Do you move with energy and purpose, or seem to be wandering adrift? It makes a big difference in terms of how you are perceived. It might surprise you that movement impacts your first impression. People who move with purpose and intention are viewed in a more positive light than people who seem aimless. One quick way to improve your movement is to make up a reason to move. For example: I'm going to retrieve a fax from the fax machine. Instead of a meaningless communication, I'll tell myself that the fax is the company president's meeting schedule, and he has just telephoned me; he is waiting on the line. This imaginary scenario makes me move quickly and purposefully to the fax machine to accomplish this task.

5. Small Talk

Small talk is important. While it may appear to be idle chatter, it's anything but. It is the way to gauge how comfortable you are talking one on one about non-work related topics. Most of us engage in small talk with 90 percent of the people we encounter. You must know how to make conversation about minor issues. There are only three *safe* topics for small talk: traffic (or transportation), weather, and sports. If you're not up to speed on the latest team standings, stick with weather and traffic. The simple goal here is to be upbeat and positive to create that great first impression.

6. Handshake

Your handshake speaks volumes about your warmth, your integrity and your self-confidence. Most everyone can tell you that a firm handshake is an essential part of a favorable impression, so why is it that a good handshake is so elusive? Here is how to master it:

4 steps to a Good Handshake

1. Open your (dry) right hand so that your thumb is pointed at the ceiling and your fingers are together and perpendicular to the floor.
2. Move your hand forward until you connect web to web with the shakee's hand.
3. Close your hand, keeping the back of your hand stiff. Apply slight pressure with your ring finger and pinky on the bottom of the shakee's hand.
4. Pump two short pumps and release their hand. Drop your hand to your side. **IMPORTANT**: Make sure that you make and maintain eye contact and a pleasant facial expression when you are shaking hands

Handshake Problems That Leave a Negative Impression

Fumbled handshakes seem like a small thing to base an impression upon. Keep in mind impressions and perceptions are based on hundred of small things, and at the same time, no less. There are several types of handshakes that leave a negative impression about you and can impact your professional image.

The Cup

The cup handshake gives the distinct impression that you don't want to touch the shaker's hand. Instead of keeping the back of your hand stiff during the close on the shaker's hand, your palm moves into a cup shape.

Practice Tip: To overcome the cup handshake, ask a friend to practice with you and attach a piece of sticky backed Velcro to your palm and theirs. Practice getting stuck together at least 20 times, then remove the Velcro and see if the cup handshake is a thing of the past.

Ladyfingers (or Damsel in Distress)

Ladyfingers handshake can be either initiated by a woman or forced upon her by a man. The outcome is the same. The hand is offered, but before web-to-web contact is made, the fingers are grasped and the hand is turned over so that the back of the woman's hand is facing the ceiling. When men have turned my hand over this way I have often had the creepy sensation that they were about to kiss my hand (in some misguided attempt at chivalry). When women present their hand this way it appears that they are either prissy or do not understand business. It gives a very negative impression.

Practice Tip: To overcome the ladyfingers handshake, ask a friend to practice with you. Attach a very small piece of sticky Velcro on your web and index finger. Attach the opposing piece of Velcro on their web and palm (opposite the thumb). Practice sticking both pieces of Velcro together before closing your fingers. Once you have closed, pump twice while perpendicular to the floor.

Premature Grasp

Less offensive than ladyfingers but still uncomfortable is the premature grasp. This fumble occurs when either party closes the fingers before making web-to-web contact. The result is a finger shake rather than a handshake.

Practice Tip: To overcome the premature handshake, ask a friend to practice with you. Attach a small piece of sticky Velcro on your web. Attach the opposing piece of Velcro on their web. Practice sticking the web-to-web Velcro together before closing your hand to shake.

Fish handed

The fish hand is the least common fumble but is unforgivable. This is when the thumb is kept close to the fingers rather than extended up to the ceiling. The result is the sensation of trying to hold on to a fish out of water.

Practice Tip: To overcome the fish handshake, ask a friend to practice with you. Put a medium thick 2"diameter rubber band around your right wrist. Twist a loop in the rubber band and slip the loop over your thumb. Point your fingers toward your partner, your thumb should now be pointing at the ceiling. Practice connecting web to web and then closing your thumb at least 50 times.

Grip O' Death

If people wince or rub their hand after you shake you may be gripping their hand much too tightly. Remember that the handshake is a social convention and not a strength contest. There are two places where the grip can be too strong. Pinching the web is a common problem or closing too strongly with the bottom fingers.

Practice Tip: To overcome the grip o' death, ask a friend to practice with you. Imagine that you are shaking hand with an egg. If you squeeze too hard the egg will crack. After you practice gently shaking their hand for 20 times, have them hold a raw egg and see if you can shake their hand without cracking the egg.

Wet Noodle

The wet noodle is a two-fold problem. One part is the perspiring hand and the second is the limp handshake. There is not much you can do to prevent the perspiration that comes from excitement or nervousness. But if you know that this is a problem for you make sure that you have a handkerchief in your suit pocket to wipe your hand on quickly. For the limp handshake, practice keeping firmness in the palm and back of your hand, and applying pressure with your ring finger and pinky.

Practice Tip: To overcome the wet noodle, ask a friend to practice with you. Imagine that your hand is made of steel. It is firm and does not crumple when squeezed. Also practice wiping your hand on a handkerchief in your suit pocket before shaking. Ask your partner if it is noticeable and work on it at least 40 times until it becomes second nature and is not noticeable.

Women's Handshake Issue

Women must initiate handshakes. Before women were an integral part of the workforce there was little reason for them to shake hands on a regular basis. Men were steeped in the cultural norm that you did not shake hands with women unless they initiated the handshake.

While the last 30 years have certainly changed the rules, there still seems to be some holdover and awkwardness with women and handshakes. Women must offer their hand to anyone they are meeting, men and women. Sometimes women shake hands with men they are meeting and then sort of wave to the women, as if to say "We know we have to do this for them but we can just wave at each other." This is unprofessional.

Women must overcome any shyness they have about shaking hands with each other. Decide that you are going shake hands with everyone that you meet or are introduced to. Knowing what you are going to do will alleviate any awkwardness because you are not having to think about what you are going to do, you already know what you are going to do and you just do it.

Visibility Value

How Are You Seen?

There are two implications to how you are seen. The first refers to how visible you are inside and outside of your organization. If you show up for work, do what you are supposed to do and leave, you may not be seen at all. You are doing what is expected, but you are not necessarily *visible.*

Being visible means that you are doing something that makes you stand apart. You are a member or perhaps the leader of a special team or task force; you volunteer to coordinate the blood drive, or you organize the company outing. You take on extra tasks that you may not be compensated for, but which will gain you recognition. Every task or activity that you volunteer to be part of adds information to other people's perceptions of you, so you should consider your activities carefully. If you are looking for added responsibility or a promotion, volunteer for the budget review committee or the management advisory group. If you volunteer only for company social activities, potlucks, holiday parties, etc. you might be perceived as socially connected and enjoying the fun stuff.

Your current job profile will impact how your volunteer efforts are regarded. For example, Sally is an administrative assistant, whose responsibilities include handling payroll, updating staff on procedures and human resources issues and scheduling departmental meetings. When she volunteers to head up the company picnic it is seen as extension of meeting planning, and she doesn't get a lot of extra credit or perception points. Jim, on the other hand, is a systems analyst who has found that no one takes much notice that he has agreed to be on call most weekends. When Jim volunteers to buy the beverages for the annual picnic he gains visibility and perception points by becoming involved in an area outside of the type of work he normally does. He was seen in a new positive light.

Visibility is key to making sure that your co-workers and supervisors consider you not only a team player but also a true asset to the organization.

Name Campaign

Learning names is one important way to get positive perception points. When you know a person's name and use it to greet her, you will be noticed. Don't let the old excuse of "I'm not good with names" defeat you. Think of it as a job skill and commit yourself to memorize the names of the people you see often.

When I was hired to assist in the grand opening of the first Nordstrom store in the Chicago area, I knew that I had low visibility, in part because I was hired in Chicago and had not transferred from another store. I also knew that after the big opening, anyone with low visibility would be expendable. So I set my mind on learning the names of all of the managers and assistant managers. Every night I'd look over my list of departments and names, each day I'd look around to see who was in each department and I'd listen to see that I had figured out the right name for the right person. When I knew I had the correct name I'd smile and say "Hi Susan" or "Good morning, Bob." They would say "Hello," but they were thinking, "Who are you?" Why do you know my name? What is your name?"

Within three months of my *name campaign* I noticed that all of the managers and most of the sales people knew my name. Did this make me more visible? YES! Did I survive the lull after our big opening? YES! I was also able to transfer to a more prestigious and lucrative department and was selected as the vice president for the Customer Service Board.

People value their name and transfer that value to those who know it, as well. Learn those names. Once I proved to myself that the names make a difference, I've made it my business to learn names quickly.

Not good with names?

Over the years I've developed a technique to help me commit names to memory. When I first meet someone I shake the person's hand, look at the face and hear the name. For me, this was too much information at one time and I'd forget the name an instant later. So now, I make sure that when I hear the name I repeat it immediately, before I let go of that hand. I also try to use people's names in conversation within two minutes of meeting them.

If it's an unusual name I ask them to spell it. Many people develop some type of mnemonic device or memory trigger to help remember names. For example, perhaps you've just been introduced to someone named "Ruth"; Ruth rhymes with booth. Picture her making a call from a telephone booth. Try associating the name and the setting. The biggest help to learning and remembering names is to *pay attention* and realize the importance of this process.

Once I recognized that knowing names contributed significantly to my visibility and potential for advancement, I stopped telling myself I was not good with names and started to perfect the skill. In my workshops participants usually remark on my ability to call them by name immediately. I study the attendance sheet prior to the session and so I feel like I'm meeting old friends when they introduce themselves to me.

Become visible in Professional Associations

You really *can* raise your visibility and propel your career by becoming an active member of professional associations. There are many reasons to volunteer your time and talents to an association. There is also much to be gained from the effort you put forth in volunteering.

Let's take a look at five reasons to become active in an association

1. **Skill development**
   Volunteer work offers an opportunity to work in capacities outside of your job description. You can develop skills you may have but don't apply to your current position, or you can learn interests and aptitudes that might have gone otherwise undiscovered.

   > *Beth Lewis, a middle school band director in Holt, Michigan, joined a professional organization. But rather than simply attend meetings of the Michigan School Band and Orchestra Association of Music Educators, she volunteered to serve as the district's treasurer, and enjoyed it so much she held the post for 7 years. "It got my name out there and I got to know everyone" as the treasurer "I learned about the organization and how it is run and how to keep it running smoothly, I also gained a lot of leadership skills and I learned about accounting – something I never would have done in my job."*

2. **Access to power**
   Volunteering through an association can give you an inside track to executives

within and outside of your company. You will cross paths with managers and other staff at higher levels or in different organizations to whom you would normally not have access. These informal contacts and the impression that you make can impact your future. Managers tend to share information in a casual way when considering candidates for promotion.

> *I first discovered how this worked when I had volunteered to organize the company picnic at Nordstrom's Department Store. To pull the event together I had to work with the restaurant manager, the store manager and the human resource manager. I might never have met them under everyday circumstances, but we were certainly all well acquainted by the close of the event. Moreover, we now shared something in common – the pleasure of bringing off a successful event.*

3. Enhanced social life

Let's face it, many of us rely on the people we work with to meet our social needs. Those you volunteer with, on the other hand, know you outside of your job. Because of your similar interests they may become lifelong friends.

Some of the benefits of volunteering and becoming involved in leadership are the trusting relationships that you develop with others that are active in the association. Rick Binford, CMP Director of Corporate Sales at Conferon and President of Michigan Meeting Professionals International, states that working with others in an association leadership role "establishes a level of trust and creates a bond that cannot be created any other way."

Peggy Kline, a professional speaker and President of the National Speakers Association; Michigan Chapter feels that her involvement in the association was greatly enhanced by her leadership experience "Leadership in an association strengthens your communication, organization and team building skills. It is empowering to bring a team together for the ultimate goal of impacting the greater good of your organization." Association leaders gain from the experience, exposure and visibility such a role provides. The educational programming, conferences and information that an association can provide is often offered for free or at a discount to the association leadership.

Finally, as Peggy Kline points out association leadership "provides an excellent opportunity to enhance your professional relationships within your association."

4. Shared passion and knowledge

Sometimes the world seems to narrow when we become adults. The sports, hobbies and extra-curricular activities that we enjoyed in our youth or were involved in as children and young adults fall by the wayside as the responsibilities of work, home and family take precedence. Though we may no longer have the ability or opportunity to play soccer, ice skate or participate in a debate tournament, we can still share our enjoyment and knowledge with others.

Sports teams, scout troops and after school clubs can all benefit from your time and experience. These youth groups need coaches, judges, leaders and fundraisers. Volunteering in these areas helps you reconnect with a part of your life that was important to you. And it is tremendously satisfying to see that your influence can have a positive impact on newcomers to the activity.

5. Gratitude

Finally, volunteering is an opportunity to give back, to show appreciation for the good things that have come to us in life. We can express our gratitude through volunteering our time, energy and experience to help others. That we are able to derive personal benefit while doing for others seems almost too good to be true.

> *"Gratitude unlocks the fullness of life. It turns what we have into enough, and more. It turns denial into acceptance, chaos to order, confusion to clarity. It can turn a meal into a feast, a house into a home, a stranger into a friend. Gratitude makes sense of our past, brings peace for today, and creates a vision for tomorrow."* – Melody Beattie

The efforts that you put forth will express your gratitude in a truly significant way and create a vision for tomorrow.

5

Business Behavior

Business Behavior and Professional Etiquette

Business behavior or professional etiquette is defined as the way you interact, treat, respect and respond to those that you work with.

Keep workplace conversation appropriate

Avoid talking about personal issues. Many people feel that the people they work with are part of their social life and therefore do not have any qualms about discussing personal issues. While this is completely understandable, it can make you appear less professional as well as less effective at work. It's best to save your personal discussions for after work or during lunchtime.

Dana was assigned to a new project and she was shocked to find that she would be sharing an 8x10 foot office with six other consultants.

"The perimeter of the room was lined with computers and we sat shoulder to shoulder with one phone for the seven of us. It was impossible not to overhear personal phone conversations, and we became so overly familiar with personal issues that it became difficult to focus."

Work becomes uncomfortable without the separation of public demeanor and private issues. Safe topics for workplace conversation include:

- Transportation/ Traffic
- Weather
- Sports

Personal questions, no matter how seemingly innocent to the person asking, can feel invasive to coworkers. Probing about personal issues does not convey a professional image, and in some cases, may even open your organization to litigation.

Monitor your complaints

If you have a complaint about your work, make sure that you complain upwards to your supervisor or to your manager, and never across to your coworkers or down to subordinates.

Even though good-humored complaining may feel like you're just venting, and contributing to cohesiveness within the work environment, it often creates long-term problems.

Complaints breed dissatisfaction. Once the cycle has begun, it is sometimes difficult to stop, and the complaints spiral to include all aspects of your work, co-workers, your office setting, salary and so on. This behavior, in addition to being unprofessional, is very destructive. It can damage your credibility and give you a reputation for being the whiner in the office. When you publicly complain, you create an opportunity for someone else. Others may try to 'help' by taking on extra responsibilities, problem-solve for you, or even take your position. When you are heard complaining, your negativity shines a light on those who view circumstances more positively.

> *"I thought I was just airing my grievances and that my friends were being supportive. I remember one particular occasion when I was complaining about having to set up the logistics for training classes, my assistant asked me if I'd like him to take care of setting up the training rooms and scheduling classes. I was thrilled and it didn't take long for me to offload some other responsibilities on him as well because whenever I complained he offered to help me out. Without my realizing it he had taken on my entire job and less than a year later I was looking for work and he had been promoted into my job."*

Nancy's experience may not be typical, however it proves my point: when you repeatedly complain down to your subordinates, it affects their morale. Plus, you imply that you expect your staff to appease your complaints by taking on whatever tasks you're complaining about. Again, it is best not to complain at work but if you must, make sure that you complain in the right direction.

Never complain about your boss

If you must complain about your boss, complain only to your spouse or your pet, because your spouse wants you to keep your job and your pet won't tell! Everybody else will tell a friend at work (even though they swear they

45

won't) and information like that is certain to get back to the person on top. If you have a complaint about your boss, make sure you don't voice it to even a very close colleague. If a coworker can score some points by letting a little something slip, they may not be able to resist.

Meeting Etiquette

Our workplaces are overrun with meetings. People have meetings to prepare for meetings! It is best to schedule meetings only when it is absolutely necessary to have all the players in the room to make a decision. Provide an agenda with time schedules and expected outcomes for the meeting. Many times I've gone to meetings where no one in the room seemed to know why they were there, what we we're meeting about, or who called us together.

Agendas

Meetings without agendas and/or expected outcomes often drift off-track and end up causing confusion and frustration. This practice is extremely wasteful. If you totaled the salaries of the people in the room for those hours, you would discover that you are burning thousands of dollars along with human energy that could be spent getting work done. If you are the one calling the meeting, be sure to prepare a clear agenda that identifies the issues to be discussed and decisions that you hope to reach. Make sure everyone has a copy of the agenda and that you stick to it.

Timeliness and preparation are key

Another sign of being a professional is that you are on time and prepared to contribute to the meeting. If you are leading the meeting you must ensure that you begin and end the meeting on time. Meetings should end with a recap of the decisions made, actions to be taken, and review those persons responsible for the taking action.

Meeting archetypes

I've spent many hours attending meetings, and I've noticed a few archetypal attendees. See if you recognize anyone you know in these descriptions. (Keep in mind that the images that these particular individuals are displaying are **not** the professional image to which you aspire!)

The White Rabbit

"I'm late, I'm late for very important date!" The White Rabbit is never on time for meetings and is always rushing in the door, at least 10 minutes late, spilling coffee while setting down an armload of papers. "Sorry I'm late" the White Rabbit breathlessly whispers. White Rabbits expect sympathy and understanding from everyone as well as appreciation for how busy and important they are.

The greatest problem with White Rabbits is that they force a recap of information already discussed and sometimes raise questions that have already been answered or objections to issues that have already been discussed. So everyone has to break momentum in order to get them up to speed. The other issue is that most

White Rabbits are high status and truly are over-booked and therefore must be caught up before a meeting can move forward.

The Dreamer
The dreamer seems to come to meetings only because s/he needs a break from work. You'll often see dreamers either doodling sleepily onto a pad of paper or actually nodding off. Dreamers sometimes wake from their naps to fight over an issue or idea that they are somehow invested in, but it is hard to take them seriously because they've been distracted during much of the discussion.

Dreamers are embarrassing to everyone because it is difficult to know whether you should engage or ignore them. Tolerating dreamers at a meeting sends a clear message to the rest of the team that meetings have little value, unless you need to catch up on your rest. To address this problem, the meeting chair must take the dreamer aside after the meeting. The chair should seriously consider whether the dreamer should be invited to future meetings. In addition, the chair might suggest a doctor's appointment to determine whether there is a sleep-related disorder.

The Chomper
The Chomper brings food to meetings and feels free to chomp, chew and masticate his way through the discussions. At one standing meeting I frequently attended there was a great deal of competition to avoid sitting directly across from

the chomper, who in addition to much lip smacking, enjoyed talking while eating, Rather than deal with the offender directly, meeting participants made a point of sitting where they would not be confronted with "see-food." Eating during meetings is a no-no, unless it is a brown bag meeting or food has been provided at the meeting.

The Sipper

The sipper is a cousin of the chomper. Sippers bring a soda or water bottle everywhere they go, (you never know when you may dehydrate). The soda sipper seems to enjoy the "hissssss" sound that their soda makes when they screw open the cap for a sip. The water sipper creates a distraction by unscrewing and screwing the cap of their water bottle. Both the water and soda sippers generally need a bathroom break during the meeting.

The PDA Addict

In addition to developing ability to type with your thumbs, PDA's are all the rage and a terrific work tool. You may be a Blackberry user. You may know a Blackberry user. But the wonderful technology that allows those with the devices to be in constant contact with email can also lead to some disrespectful and annoying meeting behavior.

In a meeting, the PDA user often offers to email someone for an answer about an issue being discussed in the meeting. But if that person has an answer the group needs, s/he should be at the meeting as well. PDA users are in the habit of scrolling through and answering email instead of listening to issues being discussed in a meeting.

If you're calling the meeting, you set up the rules. Make it clear to participants that the information that is being shared in the meeting must take priority over other forms of communication for that time period.

Meal etiquette

We often share meals with the people we work with. Following proper etiquette while eating is important to your professional image. Proper meal etiquette is so important that many interviews are conducted over a meal so that the prospective employer can observe candidates' behavior during a meal.

A business meal is defined as eating with coworkers, casually during lunchtime, or a business meeting that takes place during a meal. In either situation, you should be aware that perceptions are always being formed about you, and your mealtime behavior is being noticed.

What to Avoid

Do not order messy foods such as spaghetti or ribs. Avoid anything that you need to eat with your fingers. You should not touch your food with your hands. Even foods that are traditionally considered finger foods, such as

French fries and fried chicken must all be eaten with a fork. If you cannot manage to eat these foods with a fork, then save them for a time that is not a business meal. Of course, if you are with colleagues at a fast food restaurant it is nearly impossible to not eat with your hands. Burgers and fries are not suited to utensils.

People seldom gather at a business meal for nourishment. They are there to socialize and share information. Manners are important. If you are not aware of traditional table manners you may want to consider hiring a business or image coach who can assist you with business dining and table manners. At the workshops that I teach, I've been surprised at the number of times participants have pointed out dining mistakes and annoyances to their work colleagues.

Manners Reminder

Here is a rundown of the manners that "mother may have taught you." Perhaps you will be reminded of something that you forgot or learn something new.

- When you are seated at your place put your napkin on your lap. Once your napkin in on your lap it must stay there and not on the table until the meal is complete
- Keep your water glass above your knife, to the right of your plate

- Break your bread in half (with your hands) before buttering
- Butter and bread should be placed on your bread plate
- Cut large pieces of lettuce in a salad into bite-sized chunks.
- Do not begin eating until everyone is served. If some are having salads before the main course, make sure all salads are served; the same is true for entrees and dessert.
- Do not lower your head down and "vacuum" up your food; remember that this is a social event and you should take breaks from eating to participate in conversation
- Do not chew with your mouth open
- Do not talk with food in your mouth
- If there is something that you must spit out, (olive pit or chicken bone) put your napkin to your mouth to discretely remove the object and wrap it in your napkin
- Do not discuss body functions of any kind at the table
- If a type of food gives you indigestion, don't mention it
- Ask others to pass items to you rather than reaching across the table
- Keep your elbows off of the table
- Never lick your fingers
- Use a knife to help you get food onto your fork; never use your fingers

- If wine is a part of the meal, limit yourself to one glass; do not risk becoming uninhibited or impairing your judgment
- Cut food with your knife and fork rather than the side of your fork
- Pace yourself, so that you will finish eating approximately at the same time as others at the table
- Once you have finished your meal, do not "pick" at food or eat anything else from your plate
- Place your knife and fork diagonally across your plate (11 o'clock and 5 o'clock position) to let the server know you are done eating
- Leave anything that you cannot finish at the restaurant. While it is becoming common to box up a part of a meal to go home, it is inappropriate to take a "doggy bag" home from a business lunch.

Meal etiquette mistakes can undo the credibility you've established at work. On the other hand, good etiquette during business meals creates an opportunity to reinforce your professional image. Besides, using appropriate manners are a way of making others feel comfortable.

When I spoke about waiting until everyone was served during a session of my professional image workshop, a group at one of the tables broke into laughter. They pointed at one of their coworkers and said, "he's done before the rest of the plates hit the table." The participant pleaded ignorance. He had never learned that it is civilized to wait until everyone was served before beginning (or in his case, finishing!) his meal.

6

Appropriate Appearance

Appearance

To increase your visibility and improve how you are seen professionally, it is important to consider appearance. Although each workplace is unique, and may have differences in what is acceptable in terms of appearance, there are some ironclad rules you must follow. You cannot change the fact that others will make judgments about you based on external factors. You _can_ control the external factors.

The external factors of appearance include wardrobe - clothing, shoes, accessories; and grooming - hair, skin, fingernails, and teeth. The use of appropriate clothing and grooming to present a professional image is important for several reasons, including creating and fostering a sense of commonality in the work environment, eliminating distractions, and making a much more favorable impression.

Wardrobe

In the late 1970's, John Malloy wrote a book called _Dress for Success_ that prescribed a "uniform" for looking your best in corporate America. His suggestions included specific, conservative dress requirements for both men and women. Although the days of blue suits and red paisley looped ties may be gone, dressing appropriately for work should not be forgotten.

Today, dressing for success means that you are aware of your appearance and dress appropriately. Dressing for success means dressing for the position you want - not the position you have. This last point is tricky because sometimes a manager or supervisor may perceive your appearance as a challenge (if you are consistently wearing a jacket and she is not). In that case, dress as well as, but not better than, your supervisor, and pay attention to grooming.

Dressing for the job you want – not the job you have -- can be challenging if you have to wear a uniform. A hospital security guard had an effective way of dressing for the job that he wanted, despite this constraint. Each day he came to work in a shirt, tie and sport coat and went to the employee locker room to change into his security guard uniform. Before he left work each day he changed back into his sports coat, shirt and tie. He did get some teasing at first – but the speed with which he was promoted put an end to that. Was he promoted because he looked the part? Or did his appearance contribute to his professional behavior and lead him to be promoted because of his behavior? You decide!

It's not the fact that you wear a jacket or that the security guard wears a tie that is important. It is the very subtle shift that occurs in how you are perceived based on your appearance. A number of participants in my workshops have stated that when they are wearing a jacket or are dressed in a professional manner they feel more serious about their work.

The consistency of that appearance is important too. If you wear a suit one day, jeans the next and then a sweater and slacks, you appear inconsistent and perhaps insecure. You may be doing more damage to your image than if you wear khakis and a sports shirt each day.

How Business Casual Made Business, Casual

When companies decided to change their dress code from formal business attire to business casual it was a short hop from Dockers™ and sweaters to jeans and overalls – or worse, low-cut after hours social attire.

Early in my career I worked as a consultant for Ford Motor Company. It was the bastion of the blue suit and red tie. As the company embraced teamwork as the overriding operating philosophy they began an effort to break down the supervisor/subordinate infrastructure and move toward a more inclusive and approachable team environment. In the spirit of teambuilding, the company implemented a business casual dress code. The dress code was phased in over a period of weeks, and at the same time the management dining rooms were eliminated to create a more egalitarian atmosphere.

Fast forward 10+ years: The business casual dress code made the gap between the various levels of management and workers even more conspicuous, because business casual attire has a wider range of variety. Executives are now wearing very expensive casual clothing and the difference between moderate and expensive casual wear is more evident than the difference between a moderately priced blue suit and an expensive designer label blue suit. For example, when the business casual dress code was implemented many managers and workers began to wear a shirt and sweater combination. The executives however began wearing very distinctive hand knit sweaters from Australia that ranged in price from $200 – $500. So even though everyone in the office is wearing sweaters, the clothing differential is as apparent as ever. Some organizations are considering returning to a more formal dress code.

One of the problems with a business casual dress code, as many organizations can attest, is that it is somewhat vague and open to interpretation. What I perceive as casual wear, you may perceive to be grungy, garage cleaning wear; what you perceive as business wear, I might perceive as a party outfit. Many companies have found that they need to have a much more detailed dress code to clarify what is and is not appropriate for work. I have seen staff come to work in what appears to be pajamas, but they are still within the dress code.

Companies have found that allowing employees to dress in a business casual way has not increased productivity, teamwork or camaraderie – it has in many cases just made business – casual.

If your office standard is business casual, you cannot come to work in a suit each day; you will be out of sync with your colleagues. You can however project a professional image by presenting a consistent, neat, coordinated and business suitable look.

Wardrobe Basics

How do you ensure a business suitable look? Start by looking at magazines, catalogs and people you admire to compile a list of items that you'd like to have and a professional style that you are working toward. Examine the contents of your closet and give away or put away anything that is not consistent with a professional image.

Quality not Quantity

Quality matters. This means that the fabric, cut and details of your clothing are important and noticeable. Natural fabrics such as wool and cotton generally hold their shape and feel better than synthetics such as rayon. Stitching is an important detail. Small even stitches and seams that are pressed flat are details that make a difference and contribute to the overall look of a piece.

Build Around 2 or 3 Colors

The fastest and most economical way to build a professional wardrobe is to start with basic colors such as black, tan, navy or gray, and add different bottoms or change blouses or shirts. Once you have a good foundation of basic colors it is easy to update your wardrobe with a bright jacket or colorful tie. With a good quality wardrobe of basic colors you can add colorful accessories to change your seasonal look.

Tailor Business Clothing

Many retailers have tailoring onsite and will shorten sleeves and slacks on full price items at no extra charge. Most menswear stores offer tailoring; unfortunately, women's clothiers do not always make alterations available. If the store you shop at does not offer alterations you will have to find a tailor. Bridal shops and dry cleaners are good sources to check when looking for a tailor. Independent tailors and franchises are listed in the Yellow Pages. Men are accustomed to having clothing tailored but many women overlook the importance of this step in building their wardrobe. You may spend several hundred dollars on a jacket but if the sleeves are too long, you have undermined your professional look.

Two for One

A common mistake is to buy a suit or outfit and only wear the pieces together. If you buy a two- or three-piece suit, think of each piece as a separate. If it can only be worn as an outfit, pass it up. When you are making a purchase, determine whether the pieces can be worn separately with another part of your wardrobe. Hang the jacket, skirt or slacks on separate hangers in the closet to help you remember to pair them with other things.

Jackets Are a Focal Point

Power and authority - that's what a jacket says. Spend the most on your jackets and buy the best you can afford. They are the focal point for your wardrobe. Nice shirts, sweaters and blouses can be found at many discount retailers, so spend the majority of your clothing budget on sport coats, blazers or jackets. High quality, well-tailored jackets can be paired with many shirts, sweaters and various slacks and/or skirts to give you versatility in addition to a professional, polished look.

Shoes Must be in Good Condition and Polished

Shoes matter and the quality of the shoes reflects the professionalism of the wearer. Keep your shoes polished and in good repair. Constant wear is hard on your shoes, so if you have a pair that you like to wear every day, buy a duplicate pair so you can switch off. Men's shoes have come a long way. Wingtips were at one time the only acceptable dress shoe, but there are many styles of dressy options for men now. Women's shoes continue to change style frequently. For a professional image, heel height for women should not exceed 2 ½ inches. Sling back heels and mules continue in popularity but women should wear closed toe shoes for work. Sandals or sneakers are never acceptable for a professional image.

Leg Covering

Since we're on the issue of shoes, we must discuss leg covering, a.k.a. socks and hosiery. It is important to always wear some type of socks or hosiery to work. There has been a recent trend toward bare feet or bare legs and shoes to the office, but this is one of the areas where business casual has gone too far. Many state laws require individuals to wear some type of "foot-covering" between feet and shoes at work. If you find pantyhose uncomfortable, choose an alternative such as knee-highs or thigh highs. Sometimes I hear that it is difficult to wear socks or hosiery with sandals; my response is that sandals are too casual for work anyway. There is a time and a place for everything, and work is the time and the place to wear leg and foot coverings out of respect for your colleagues, your position and the work environment.

Update eyewear

Styles change in eyewear as quickly as in other areas of fashion, and yet this is one area that is often overlooked with regard to professional image. Glasses that are too large, too small or dated in some other way will detract from your image. If possible purchase glasses that reflect the latest style, and upgrade to "no line" bifocals or thinner lenses. Glasses are an accessory that contributes to your appearance every day so it pays to purchase the most comfortable and fashionable pair possible.

Consistency

As mentioned at the beginning, consistency in appearance is important. If you wear a suit one day, jeans the next and then a sweater and slacks on the third, you may be doing as much damage to your image as wearing khaki's and a tee shirt.

One habit that I see some women get into is what I call "costuming." Rather than evolving a consistent look and sticking with it, they wear different "costumes" each day. Tuesday projects, "I'm a serious business woman in my gray pin-stripe suit." Wednesday suggests, "I'm dressed for a Caribbean cruise in my floral shirt and pink Capri's." Thursday's soft floral dress reminds me of "Little Bo Peep – have you seen my sheep?" and so on. Consistency is key to sending a message that you are serious and responsible.

How to Start Building Your Wardrobe

Not sure of what the difference is between ready to wear, moderate, designer and couture clothing? If you are serious about presenting yourself in a professional wardrobe, your first task is to become familiar with the various levels of clothing and the distinction between them. Retailers such as Nordstrom, Neiman Marcus, and Marshall Fields, among others, have very knowledgeable sales staff that will be happy to take you through the ins and outs of various clothing. And all of these larger retailers also offer a personal shopper service, if you feel intimidated about approaching the sales staff. Personal shoppers receive commission just like the sales staff. Of course the store and the shopper are hoping that you will buy something, but you are not required to, and there is no hourly fee for working with these professionals.

Benefits of Personal Shoppers

One of the benefits of building a relationship with personal shoppers or sales professionals is that they can keep an eye on sales and notify you if and when an item that you admire is marked down. They will keep a file of your sizes and preferences and can have a fitting room stocked with the appropriate styles and sizes for you to try on if you call in advance, saving you time and aggravation. Personal shoppers in my experience are also very honest, and will tell you if something does not look right on you by gently suggesting another outfit. Personal shoppers and sales professionals rely on establishing credibility with their clients for their future sales. It's not worth it to them to be less than honest with you about your choices.

Another advantage of personal shoppers is their familiarity with various fabrics, styles, and the small details like double stitching that can help educate you about what to look for whether at their stores, a designer discount store or upscale consignment shop.

Personal shoppers are available for both men and women and you may need to give more than one a try before you find the right chemistry. As with anything, don't give up on the first try – the right personal shopper is well worth pursuing.

Business Suitable

The fact that your company has a business casual dress code does not mean that anything goes. It is important to keep the following information in mind:

Informal does not mean unkempt

Unkempt means disheveled, and scruffy. There is nothing that will shout unprofessional more quickly than a rumpled appearance. If you are not willing or able to iron your clothing for work, send it out for laundering. Appearing as if you slept in your clothing will undo the hard work that you perform at your job.

Stylish and put-together

Business casual clothing may be more comfortable and less confining – but it should still appear stylish and coordinated. Compatible colors, quality fabric and proper fit are even more important when you are dressing in a more casual way.

No jeans or sneakers

Jeans, no matter how pricey the label, are not appropriate for the office. Denim in general is not acceptable, even on casual Fridays. Sneakers belong in your gym locker, not in the workplace.

Tips For Women

It important not to appear sexy at work. You are there to work, not to attract sexual attention. That means not showing skin (cleavage or stomach). Skirts should cover the top of the knee and end mid knee or just below the kneecap. Blouses should be sturdy and made from opaque material – no bra or camisole straps showing through. Tops made with Lycra™ should be avoided as they hug the body tightly.

Natural cotton, linen or silk dresses, or blouses and dress slacks are a fine alternative to a suit. The blouse must be crisply pressed and have some starch, like men's shirts. (Be aware that many dry cleaners will not launder, press and starch women's shirts as they do men's, they state that they are too small and must be dry cleaned - at quadruple the price). One easy way to upgrade your appearance is to always buy slacks that are lined. The lining not only extends the life of the slacks, it gives them more body so they don't bag, sag, or cling. Lining is a sign of better quality in slacks, skirts and jackets.

Accessories can add to your overall look, but excessive accessories are likely to detract instead. Always apply the "Rule of 3" to your business casual dressing. You should limit yourself to three accessories, to avoid a cluttered, unprofessional look. Note that a fussy neckline on a blouse or dress counts as an accessory, as do eye glasses. Long dangling earrings count as double accessories. So, if you are wearing glasses, earrings, a broach and a necklace, you have now detracted from your professional image.

Tips For Men

Men must always wear a shirt that has a collar. This means that T-shirts, sweaters without shirts underneath or sweatshirts are out of the question. Many offices that have a business casual dress code still expect men to wear a long sleeved shirt and tie. Short-sleeved dress shirts may be fine for social events in warm weather, but should not be a part of your work wardrobe. If you work in an environment that calls for a short-sleeved dress shirt, skip the tie.

The best business suitable look for men who want to be promoted is a long-sleeved shirt and tie with dress slacks. Make sure that you always have a sport coat or jacket in the office in case you are called to a meeting that requires looking more professional.

Men should avoid sweater vests and patterned flannel shirts. While they may be comfortable, they do not project professionalism.

Grooming Basics

Hair: Squeaky clean, neat

Clean hair that is neat, off the face and in a suitable style contributes to your professional image. If you have problems with dandruff, a hair stylist may be able to help you find products that can help you to keep your hair clean and flake free.

Men: Aim for clean cut, preferably beardless

If you look at the men in top positions at most companies, you will see that they do not, for the most part, have facial hair. Men in academic settings, on the other hand very often have some type of beard, mustache or goatee. So again, we look at the match between who you are and what you present. If you are looking to be promoted in an organization you should model yourself after the men in the positions you are seeking. Most are clean cut and beardless.

Women: Makeup - subtle and understated

Women who are over 30 should always wear makeup to work. There, I've said it. Wearing makeup is part of presenting a professional image. Makeup should be used to enhance rather than detract. The mistake that many women commit with makeup is wearing too much eye makeup. Under age 30 should wear mascara, lip-gloss or lipstick and blush. Women over age 30 should be wearing foundation in addition to mascara, blush and lipstick to present a professional image.

Skin: clear, healthy, odorless

When it comes to considering perfume and other scents, it is best to go without. If you have a problem with excessive perspiration, you may want to consult your doctor. Odorless doesn't mean that you just don't smell of perspiration; you do not smell of cologne or perfume, as well. Many individuals are allergic to fragrances. To smell of a fragrance, even if it is pleasant for you, may impact other people and their perception of you in a negative way. Odorless also means that you do not smell of cigarette smoke, garlic, onions or have bad breath.

Fingernails: well manicured

Fingernails should be short and clean. Women are permitted longer fingernails if they are polished, manicured and maintained. Women who have fingernails that are more than an inch in length, project the image that they may not be capable of certain kinds of work because their fingernails make such work nearly impossible. How can anyone type on a computer keyboard with inch-long nails? If your nails are polished make sure that the polish is not chipped. Do not put fingernails or cuticles in your mouth while at work. Nail biting looks juvenile, and spreads germs to colleagues unfortunate enough to shake your hand or borrow a pen.

Hair Today, Gone Tomorrow

"So, what have you got against hair?" a colleague asked me. I don't have anything, per say, against hair, but I have seen people sabotage themselves by what they do (or don't do) with their hair.

Hair is a loaded topic. To many of us it is our crowning glory, and we spend a great deal of time thinking about it, coloring it, straightening or curling or cutting it. Yet rarely do I hear people wondering, "does the style I've chosen suit me and the position I want to be in?"

A woman I'll call Kelly had extremely curly hair and was in my professional image seminar. She had all of her hair piled in a ponytail on top of her head. She acknowledged that it looked less than professional. Her goal was to become a supervisor, but her "Pebbles" cartoon hairdo sent the message that she was young and immature. Kelly said she didn't know of any hairstylist that could style her hair. I knew of a manager who had the same type of coarse curly hair and obtained the name of her stylist. When I ran into Kelly several weeks later and asked if she had called for an appointment she said that she had decided that her hair was okay and she didn't want to change it. She has been turned down twice since then for the supervisor position in her department.

Hair should be neat, clean, under control and off the face. For women, the recommended professional look is shoulder length or shorter. If you are a woman and love long hair and feel it is a part of who you are, then tie it back in a bun, twist or a neat ponytail when you are at work. One of the reasons that women (and men for that matter) like long hair is that it is considered sexy – all the more reason why hair should be tied back at work. As ridiculous as it seems, there is still the perception that you cannot be sexy and professional at work at the same time.

Another reason to keep long hair up or back is the perception that long hair makes you look like a little girl (if you are under 30) or like you are trying to hang on to your youth (if you are over 40). Don't get me wrong, I think it's ridiculous to imply that hair length has a direct effect on one's careers. Hair length should be a matter of personal choice. But as we've discussed, the way we present ourselves communicates volumes of information, and you should be aware of the common perceptions about hair so that you can make smart, informed choices.

A Moment in Time

Finally, let's talk about something that no one wants to acknowledge, the frozen hairstyle. Many women, and sometimes men, find a style that suits them and then decide "this is it – I will wear this style forever." Well, styles do change over the years and a part of looking professional is looking up to date. If you have not changed your hairstyle in more than 10 years, start looking at magazines and see what is in style. Can you modify your look to reflect these changes?

Sometimes all it takes is going to a new hair stylist once in a while and using his or her expertise in what is current, and whether that look would work for you. I am not suggesting that you do a complete overhaul; if you have teased bangs that are hair sprayed up into a "poof" and the current look is straight slicked back hair, losing the bangs may be enough to really update your style.

Paper Clips vs. Hair Clips

Vicky, another workshop participant reminded me of an important, but sometimes overlooked point. Even though we were indoors, she had her sunglasses on top of her head for the entire day. Finally, I asked her why she was wearing her sunglasses on her head and she confessed that she used them as a head band! It was her regular hairstyle! A number of women in my classes have had pencils or large binder clips holding up their hair. Using appropriate hair accessories is important. "I can't be bothered" is not the impression we want to send our bosses and coworkers. Yet using office supplies for grooming purposes, that is exactly the message we are sending.

7

Professional Strategies for Interviewing

Professional Strategies for Interviewing

Up until now, we have talked about projecting a professional image on the job. But what if you are in the process of looking for a job? Needless to say, the way you look and behave on an interview is even more crucial.

I'm about to reveal one of the biggest secrets of interviewing. Deciding whom to interview is all about piles. Yes, piles.

Now, many companies have sophisticated software that screens key words – and they do use it. And they have specific criteria to help compare candidates. However, when it comes down to whom to actually interview much of the process is subjective. And that's where the piles come in. Most interviewers take the resume pool and form three piles. Maybe, No Thanks, and Yes. Those that are in the No Thanks pile usually get letters thanking them for their interest in the company; we will keep your resume on file for a year... blah blah blah. Then, the Maybe pile is looked at again and sorted into No Thanks and Yes. The Yes pile is the group that is contacted for interviews.

If you have an interview scheduled, congratulations! You have made it to the YES pile.

To stay in the YES pile, you want to do everything right at the interview. You want to avoid those behaviors or gaffes that would send you into the No Thanks pile. You want a second interview; you want to stay in the YES pile and get the job.

If you respond to an interview offer with unavailability and excuses, you may slip from Yes to Maybe. Do not let scheduling an interview become difficult. Take a sick day, hire a sitter, offer to come early or late – do whatever you have to do to stay in the Yes pile.

If you do move on to a second interview and you find yourself among top two or three candidates then the decision comes down to "fit." You and the other finalists are all equally and yet uniquely qualified for the position. Subsequent interviews are less about what you have done than about who you are and how you will meet the needs of the organization. Are you a comfortable fit? Are you going to challenge the status quo – and is that what they want?

What do you want and where do you want to end up? This is what is important at the final interviews. You need to keep selling yourself, because even if you do have doubts, you want the job offer. This is what gives you the power. Until then, you can be subjected to the No Thanks pile at any time.

The Stages of the Interview

You may think the job interview begins the moment you shake hands, take your seat, and respond to the opening question. Wrong!

As soon as anyone who is part of the organization sees or hears you, the interview is in progress. If you are terse with the security guard or appear frazzled when greeting the receptionist, the word may be passed along to your potential employer.

As a young sales consultant on my way to work at Nordstrom, I noticed an attractive woman in a red sedan behind me in the parking ramp. As I waited for a car to pull out of a parking space, she laid on the horn and then roared past me as I pulled into the vacated spot. She joined me in the elevator, still tense and glaring with indignation. The door opened, and we walked together in silence, me to the cash register and she to her interview appointment with the department manager.

Later, when the manager told me the woman had applied to work in my department, I related the garage incident. Possibly I was overly sensitive to her behavior, since I was also vice president of the Customer Service Board that year. Beyond that, it is human nature to react negatively to someone behaving rudely.

I have since learned that employees will naturally try to protect their workplace from unpleasant co-workers. On the reverse side, I would have also been inclined to put in a positive word for her, had she acted civilly.

So, here you are on the way to the interview. You're more composed than the irate woman in the red sedan, but you're also anxious for the event ahead to go well.

Take a deep breath, check your face in the rear view mirror, and smile as you exit the car. Raise your expectations that the interview will go well. Introduce yourself to the receptionist, and say "no, thank you" if you're offered a cup of coffee. He has better things to do than fetch you coffee, and you don't need another object with sloshy liquid to balance in your hands. Nor do you need to add a worry about coffee breath

And incidentally, don't assume "he" is a receptionist. In these days of downsizing, many companies have eliminated this position, assigning influential administrative assistants and other professionals to rotate managing the front desk. Treat anyone you encounter with as much respect as the person who will be interviewing you, because in reality, they are all interviewing you.

Observe your surroundings. Are there company brochures in the waiting area? Copies of the annual report? Awards posted on the wall? These items are part of the company's image. They convey how the company wants to be perceived and what it is proud of. Find something in their materials that catches your interest. Communicate your enthusiasm when the interviewer arrives to greet you.

At this point you stand, using your best posture, and extend your hand. Do not reach for your briefcase, purse or portfolio until after you've shaken hands and said hello. Remember to travel light. All you need to bring along is an extra resume, business cards, samples of your work and a wallet. You don't want to look like a packhorse, or someone ready to pitch a tent and move in.

Continue to turn down offers of coffee or water. The small talk continues as you head toward the office or conference room. But have no doubt: the interview has already begun.

It's Show Time

An interview is not just a question and answer session. It is a presentation, no less important than if you were at the podium in front of an audience. If you've ever given a speech or a presentation, you know that it consists of three sections:

- The **introduction,** during which you establish rapport and credibility with your audience
- The **body,** where you present your main points in a manner that is clear, concise and easy to follow, and
- The **conclusion**, where you summarize the speech, provide closure, and offer an action plan

An interview also includes an introduction, a body and a conclusion, and there are specific things that must happen in each section.

The introduction -- small talk

During the beginning seconds of any presentation, the speaker must set the audience expectations, forecast what the topic will be, and establish credibility by showing why you are qualified, experienced, and interested in the topic. You must give the audience a reason to listen by addressing the WIIFM question: "What's in it for *me*?"

An interview is no different. During the introduction phase known as small talk, you must establish your credibility, set expectations, appear interested and qualified, and answer the unspoken question in the interviewer's mind: WIIFM?

How do you meet all these objectives in the space of five minutes? Small talk.

Small talk may appear to be idle chatter, but it's anything but. It is the interviewer's first way to gauge how comfortable you are talking one-on-one about non-work related topics. Most of us engage in small talk with 90 percent of the people we encounter, and this is even more true in an organization. You must know how to make conversation about minor issues.

There are only three *safe* topics for small talk:
- Traffic (or transportation
- Weather, and
- Sports

If you're not up to speed on the latest team standings stick with weather and traffic.

The simple goal here is to be upbeat and positive when asked, "How was the drive?" or, "Are we ever going to get a break in this weather?" Even if you were given inaccurate directions, leading you to drive in circles for 20 minutes (still arriving on time because you wisely allowed for this possibility!) when the interviewer asks, ""did you find us okay?" your *only* response is "Yes. No problem!"

But that's lying, you say. Aren't you supposed to tell the truth at an interview? Not in this case. The purpose of small talk is never to vent complaints. It is only to lay positive groundwork.

The real purpose of small talk

As someone who has conducted hundreds of interviews with prospective employees, I'll let you in on a secret. I don't *really* care about the traffic on the expressway or how you feel about this year's record snowfall. I want to know that if you and I find ourselves riding on an elevator together, we can have a pleasant conversation. I want to be reassured that if I ask "How are you?"

you'll usually respond with "fine, and you?" rather than a litany of your physical problems. If I offer a comment about the weather, you will not begin a lecture on global warming.

What I'm really curious about is the way you react when unexpected events unfold. Is it panic and doom, or do you take them in stride? Show me an example of how you relate to strangers and colleagues. When the traffic is awful, do you get upset? Or switch gears, by taking the scenic route?

The body of the interview

This is the actual asking and answering of questions. This is when your practice and preparation will really pay off. The body of the interview contains the volley of questions and answers that the interviewer will use to determine if you will stay in the Yes pile or if you are moving toward the Maybe or No piles. One point of the questions and answers is to lead you into having a real dialogue with the interviewer. A real dialogue can only happen if you are prepared enough to ask a relevant follow-up question during the exchange and are able to then relate the information to what you know about the company and your past experience. In addition to answering questions, it's important that you pay attention to the nonverbal communication and use the REALLY technique to answer questions.

The REALLY technique

What are they REALLY Asking?

The purpose of the interview is to determine if you are a good fit for the job. There is no way to determine whether or not you are a good fit other than asking for specific information about how you handled a variety of situations in the past and where you'd like to go in the future. Many interviewers find that the interviewee is not specific and doesn't REALLY answer the question in a way that gives enough information to determine if s/he will be a good fit.

Using the acronym REALLY can help you to remember and address what the interviewer is really asking.

R- Response

When you are asked to give an example of a problem you solved, crisis you averted, or time that you dealt with a difficult customer – what is really being asked is "How effectively do you respond to a problem or crisis?" What the interviewer is looking for in asking a response question is:

1. Communication – "The first thing I did was notify my boss" or "Well, first I apologized to the customer" or " I emailed the crisis management team while I talked to the client on the phone." This answer should show that you understand the chain of

command and the importance of sharing information

2. Resolution – What steps did you take to resolve the problem? What did you do to prevent the problem from reoccurring? "I noticed that we had an emergency delivery every Friday, so I initiated a process of calling the customer for the order on Thursday, thus preventing an emergency on Friday."

E – Example

Keeping in mind that the interviewer relies on you to convince her that you are a good match for the job, you will be asked to give examples during the interview.

1. An example is a short story with relevant details that will show off your skills. "Can you give me an example of teamwork in you job?" Stating that you are on two work teams is not enough. A brief but detailed summary goes: "Well, I am currently a member of both the customer service team and the procedure team. On the procedure team we are putting together a process and procedure manual. I write and edit the first draft and then we reconvene to assign additional work," Or, "In my job we all pull together to do what we have to do to get the work done. For example, when we discovered that an order had been incorrectly submitted and the customer was in a bind because of our mistake we all

went into action. One person called the overnight shipping company and made arrangements – several of us quickly started calling other stores, one person checked our inventory and because of this type of teamwork the problem was corrected within 20 minutes and our customer was very grateful".

2. Tell the story. Storytelling is a very important skill to develop to be successful at interviews. Most of your important information will be relayed to the interviewer by telling a story. A story has a beginning, middle and end. Stories have problems that need to be solved. When the problem is resolved the ending contains the learning or moral of the story and then the update – happily ever after.

3. The beginning of your story should contain just enough background information to make the problem to be solved understandable. Clearly describe the problem without placing blame on any one particular character. (Note: your problem should be a result of a business process or system failure rather than a personal issue). Concisely describe steps you took to resolve the problem. Explain the steps and communication that you and others took to achieve a satisfactory resolution. Describe the outcome of the resolution and what was learned and improved from the process. If you have left anything out don't go back to add it; it will only add confusion. Practice

several stories until they are easy and natural to tell. Time yourself, your story should run about one minute.

Use this technique to practice telling a story. Imagine your story as a fairy tale. Start the story "Once upon a time there was a _____(character) *salesperson for this example.* Now give some detail about the character. "The salesperson was very conscientious and worked hard to make his customers happy" now here comes the set-up "One day, a customer ordered a special computer" *add detail –* "It was so special that the customer had to wait three weeks for it to be built to her specifications" *now the problem or the villain* "Finally the computer was ready and shipped to the salesperson. However, when the salesperson checked the computer it was not what the customer had ordered" *so then what?* "The salesperson called the manufacturer and explained that the computer was not right, the manufacturer said it would take three weeks to build the computer as requested again" *how does the hero (you) deal with this set back?* "So the salesperson called the customer and apologized for the problem. He offered to send the customer a better computer that was in stock for the same price" *solution offered,* "The customer was happy to get a better computer and the salesperson was able to save the sale and the customer relationship. *And they all lived happily ever after.*

This may seem silly but it's an effective way to make sure that the details, problem, solution and happy ending that you need to describe during an interview are identified and related. Thinking of the example as a fairy tale will also help to keep the details at the right level – not so detailed that you spend excessive time orienting the listener to the specifics, and not so general that the story lacks a point.

A - Action

The descriptions of the actions you took bring your stories to life. Exactly what action did you take to improve your company? If you have a portfolio or work samples, bring them to the interview to show how your actions resulted in tangible materials. Communicate action that you took to solve problems. "I worked with the shipping department to make sure the order went out immediately" or "I called 20 other locations to find the item and had it sent out the next day" or "I coordinated the different departments to make sure that the order did not fall through the cracks again.

L – Learning

What learning opportunities have you pursued? How have you kept your skills up to date? How have you improved your skills; what kind of training/education have you had and what do you still need? What have you learned from problems that you resolved?

> "So while the parts were shipped on time, we discovered that we needed a process to consistently check the voice mail 5 minutes before leaving each day" or "The customer was OK with the resolution but we realized we needed a customer service swat team" or "My boss was happy with the solution but I now have a personal checklist so that it won't happen again."

L - Leaving

Demonstrate loyalty by never speaking negatively about your current or former employer(s). Be prepared to answer concisely and positively "Why are you leaving your current position?" Employers understand leaving for greater responsibility, better opportunity, etc. Do not mention anything negative regarding your boss, co-workers or the direction of the company. Also be prepared to identify during your answers what it is that you like about your current position. That will help to determine whether or not this position is a good fit. Relate how this job will provide you the opportunity to do what you are good at and what you like to do.

Y- Yes

Interviewers do not like rejection any more than job seekers. Reassure the interviewer that if offered the job you will say Yes! Describe why you believe that you are a good match for the company and the position. Say Yes to the interviewer and chances are good they will say YES to you.

Closing the interview

You've made it through the body of the interview and now the interviewer asks "Do you have any questions for me (us)?" And the answer is... "Yes, I do have a couple of questions." The questions you ask are going to be job and company related. They will NOT be "gimme" related, i.e., focused on you.

Yes Questions (job & company focus)

- What is the direction of the company?
- How does this job support the company mission and goals?
- What is the career path for this position?
- Why is this position available?

No Questions (gimme focus)

- What is the salary?
- What type of benefits do you have?
- Is there tuition reimbursement?
- How much vacation time will I get?

Gimme questions are anything to do with what *you* will get. This includes tuition reimbursement, health insurance, bonuses and especially salary. Remember you are saying, "Yes" and are not out for what the company will provide you, but what you have to offer the company. "But I can't take a job without health insurance" you may think, and of course you can't – but you must wait. When they say "Yes" to you by offering the job, *that* is the time to talk about and negotiate benefits – never before the job offer. Repeat after me: "never before the job offer!"

What are the questions that you are going to ask? You are going to ask questions that demonstrate your intelligence and display your interest in the job. These include, what the job entails, who you will report to, how the job fits in with the overall structure of the company.

The best questions to ask are those that occur to you as a result of the dialog you been engaging in with the interviewer. Prepare at least two questions before the interview – in case none occur to you at that time.

10 compelling questions to ask

Q: *Why is this position available?*
You are asking to see if this is a new position, a position that is open due to a promotion or if someone left the company. While

it is difficult and sometimes dangerous to make assumptions based on limited information, the best scenario for you is that someone was promoted out of this position. With a new position there are sometimes unclear expectations about what can and cannot be accomplished in the new role. If someone has left the company, it could be a red flag that you need to follow up on the reasons for the departure.

Q: *Who will I report to?*

You are not looking for a name of an individual as much as the position. It is important to make sure that you will be reporting to only one manager or supervisor. If the company is planning to split your time between two areas you should be very wary, as both supervisors will invariably expect a full time effort – even though they recognize that your time is split.

Q: *Can you describe a typical day or week for someone in this position?*

Just as the company is looking for a good fit for their position, remember that you are looking for a good fit for your personality and goals as well.

I asked this question while being interviewed with a very large, well-known Fortune 500 company. I was completing my Master's degree in communication, focusing on training and development. The description made it clear to me that I would be in the sales branch of this company. The typical day involved traveling to several grocery stores to check product placement and work with the store manager on more favorable placements. The only career path was in sales. I said yes through out the interview, but after much thought afterward, decided this was not a particularly good fit for my personality and goals.

Q: What is the overall structure of the company?

You should have an inkling of this answer from the research that you have done on the company prior to the interview. It is important to understand which division you will be working with and how that relates to other units in the company. While you may have a rough idea of some key players from your research, you must make sure that you do not "show off" your research or sound as though you know what's what. You don't! (Yet!).

Q: Where do you see the company heading in the next 5 years?

Just as you must do your research about the company, you must also do your research about the industry. This is not the time to flaunt your research, but you don't want to appear extremely surprised by trend information. This question also indicates that you have a long-term commitment to the position you are seeking.

Q: Do you see major changes ahead for the company?

Pay attention to this answer for a preview of what is or is not on the horizon for your future.

This is the type of information that can help you determine your personality fit and whether or not this company will provide an opportunity for you to move toward your goals.

Q: Are these changes related to trends in the industry?

This follow-up question depends on what was stated as a response to the previous question. Besides determining what is driving the changes on the horizon, this is a good opportunity to understand what type of change management is being used to prepare the company to move forward.

Q: What is the typical career path for this position?

You need to have some idea what to expect in terms of career direction. On the other hand, do not put too much stock in the answer. While it may be true that everyone in this position has gone on to -- oh, lets say -- an operations position, that doesn't mean that you must follow that same path. If the path cannot be changed and it is unacceptable to you, do not say "No Thanks" at the interview but add this information into your decision-making process.

Q: What type of team will I be working with?

This question is to elicit information and also to reinforce with the interviewer that you are a team player and used to working in a team environment.

By phrasing the question this way, you will also be able to get a sense of whether or not the company really works in teams or just uses that terminology to camouflage a more traditional reporting structure.

Q: *How would you define success in this position?*
This will encourage the interviewer to be specific in identifying what the company is really looking for. Listen carefully, and then relate one *brief* anecdote or example (that you haven't used yet) to reinforce to the interviewer how your experience has given you the ability to meet their definition of success.

Establishing follow-up opportunities

When you are done asking questions and listening to the responses, the interviewer will generally ask, "Is there anything else?" Take the opportunity to say, "Yes" and establish follow-up opportunities and avenues.

Establishing follow-up lays the groundwork for the post-interview phase of the process.
"I don't have any more questions at the moment, but may I call or email you if I think of anything later?" Nearly every interviewer will agree to this request, so you have now been granted permission to get your name in front of them again.

So...the questions have been asked and answered, and you have established an avenue for the next steps. Now you must face the hardest moment of all. You must ask for the job.

Asking for the job is another way of saying, "Yes" to the interviewer. Asking for the job is not a pathetic plea for employment. It is a confident, *well-rehearsed* verbal recap of the interview.

- *Interviewer:* "Well, thank you for coming in today"
- *You:* "I've enjoyed meeting you and hearing about the position. I believe I'm a good match and would really like to be a part of this team."

Say this while you are still seated. If you miss the chance, and the interviewer has already stood up, then stand, shake hands, and say it. You want to ask for the job while you still have the interviewer's attention and eye contact. So pause, shake, and say, "yes" one more time. Then politely and confidently gather your briefcase and leave.

Though the official interview has concluded, remember that you are still on stage as long as anyone in the company (even the parking lot attendant) can see you. Nor is the process complete until you do follow-up. So don't drive home and kick off your shoes just yet!

Review and Thank-You

Before starting your car, or perhaps at some intermediate stop on the way home, take out your notebook and jot down anything you want to remember from your interview. In particular, note names of people you met and highlights of what you learned about the job. Then, within 24 hours, prepare and mail your thank-you letter.

The thank-you letter is a   form of business correspondence, bearing no   similarity to the handwritten note you send to the hosts of a dinner party or to your aunt acknowledging a birthday gift. It   is always typewritten on 8 ½ x 11 stationery. It can serve several functions:

- It acknowledges your appreciation
- It shows that you understand social protocol
- It reminds the interviewer of your qualifications, interest and enthusiasm
- It absolutely keeps you in the YES pile.

8

Polish Your Presentation Skills

Polish your presentation skills

As important as it is to project professionalism in your everyday work, it is absolutely critical on those occasions when you are "on stage. Whether you are discussing a sensitive issue with your manager, presenting information at a meeting of colleagues, or giving a formal presentation to the board of directors, strong presentation skills are one of the hallmarks of a true professional.

There are many courses and seminars available to improve your presentation skills but let's take a look at a few tips and techniques that you could incorporate immediately to polish your presentations.

Organization

One of the keys to a good presentation is organization. But before you begin to organize the information, think about who will be in the audience. How interested are they in what you have to say? Are they already familiar with the topic or do you have to bring them up to speed? These are factors to consider as you identify your objective for the presentation. Are you hoping to persuade a group to adopt your idea? Provide information about the status of a project? Or alert them to a new trend?

Once you clarify the objective and assess audience that you will be presenting to, it is time to look at the information that you want to cover and break it into 3 or 4 main points.

The Body

The body of the presentation is crafted from these main points or categories of information. Each main point can have several sub points. The sub points provide examples, details, statistics and other specifics that support the main point.

As an example, let's say that you have been asked to give a presentation about a new process for handling customer returns. You will be giving this presentation to your peers on the management team, so you can assume that they have some understanding of the current process and will be very interested in the specifics and details of the new process. Your objective is to inform them about the changes and convince them to use the new process. So the main points and sub points of your presentation may look like this:

1. The current customer return process is not providing the information we need (Main Point)
   a. Customer can return for any reason (sub point)
   b. Since we're not tracking reasons, we have no chance to correct the mistakes (sub point)

     c. Returns are increasing and we cannot identify the reason for this trend (sub point)

2. A new customer return process is urgently needed. (Main Point)
     a. Policy that customer can return for any reason will be unchanged (sub point)
     b. Staff assisting customer asks for return reason and assigns return code when creating return authorization (sub point)
     c. Staff enters return reason code into database along with additional information about the return (sub point)

3. This new customer return process has many benefits. (Main Point)
     a. Front line staff can offer a resolution if return reason is known (sub point)
     b. Management team can review return reasons weekly or monthly to determine if there is an issue that needs to be addressed (sub point)
     c. Trends will be easier to spot and data collection will allow us to determine various customer groups and problems or issues that lead to returns (sub point)

If you were discussing this issue in a staff meeting and organized your message according to this outline, you would appear much more professional and convincing than if you were to simply start discussing how difficult it is to determine why customers are returning our products.

Now that the main points and sub points are organized you can easily see where you fill in the sub points with specific information, examples and details.

The next step is to create the introduction and conclusion that will wrap around the body.

The Introduction
The introduction of any presentation has a number of purposes:
- It establishes your credibility
- Gives the audience a reason to listen by explaining what's in it for them
- Catches the audience's attention with an example or story about the topic
- Previews the main points of the presentation and the order in which they will be discussed.

In looking at our previous example, the introduction for that presentation may look something like this:

> *"Last week I was out of town visiting my mother. She mentioned needing some new clothes so decided to surprise her with a bright colorful jogging suit. I bought the correct size but when she tried it on, the pants were too large and the jacket too small. When I returned the suit, the sales*

associate asked me the reason for the return and then made sure to document it in her system. She stated that the buyers would be looking at that information to determine if other customers were having this problem. This could influence whether they bought merchandise from that particular company again. As the customer service manager of our company I had to ask myself, why we are not collecting similar information to make decisions that affect our business. So, I would like to take this opportunity to discuss how we currently process our customer returns, what I believe a new process could and should look like, and the benefits of changing our process for both our customers and our bottom line."

The Conclusion

The conclusion essentially serves to summarize what you have discussed. The conclusion is also the point at which you tell your audience what action you'd like them to take "Call your senator" or "Support this project." Good conclusions also often "wrap" or reference the example or story that you used in the introduction to get their attention. Finally, the conclusion ends your presentation with control. You know what your last line is and after you say it, you stop talking. Using our previous example, let's look a possible conclusion:

"As we continue to strive toward providing better customer services, it's important to recognize and change processes

that are not moving us in that direction. By changing our customer return process, we can gather relevant information and use that information to ensure we are producing what our customer needs at the quality they expect. While my mother may have been disappointed that her outfit did not fit, I'm confident that when I go back to that store they will have resolved the issue. We owe the same type of concern and caring to our customers and these changes will help us to become a more proactive and responsive organization."

Practice

Now that your presentation is well organized, it is time to focus on practicing the presentation. Practice can greatly improve your presentation and boost your confidence. Yet few people understand how to go about practicing a presentation. Practice does not mean that you read over your notes a number of times or that you mumble your main points over and over on the way to your presentation.

To get real benefit from practicing you must "stand it up." Find an empty office, conference room or living room. Send your family away and practice by standing up and giving your presentation out loud. To really get the most out of your practice session, use a timer and a tape recorder or video camera. Actors, musicians, dancers and athletes all do this. They are well aware of the importance of practice. Actors

106

practice a play for at least 6 weeks before feeling prepared to step in front of an audience, so why is it that many of us will get up and give a presentation that impacts our professional image and think that we can "wing it?" I think sometimes people are shy about practicing. They are afraid someone will overhear them and laugh, or they feel silly speaking aloud to an empty room, or they think they don't really need it.

Practice can alleviate the nervousness that accompanies many presentations. Yet as one of my workshop participants admits:

> *"When I practice I have the chance to screw up and fix my presentation a number of times before I get it just how I want it. On occasions when I haven't practiced, I often feel like I want to grab back the words coming out of my mouth and rephrase or refine them to make my point more concisely. I know that practicing improves my presentations and improves my overall professional image."*

If you can bear to tape-record or video tape your presentation, you will notice small ways in which you can work on adding vocal variety and checking your vocal tone. Listen for overused "crutch" words such as "You know" or "Like" that diminish your authority.

These "filler" phrases take focus off of what you're really trying to say, so pay attention and work to eliminate them from your presentation.

Present

On the day of your presentation or moments before it, try to get a few seconds alone to compose yourself and prepare your mind. It is important to warm up physically and vocally before presenting:

Physical Warm Ups

- Physical warm-ups: Stretch both hands high in the air, alternate hands reaching higher.
- Tilt neck side to side with shoulders down.
- Tip head front, chin on chest and then back looking at sky.
- Bring both shoulders up to ears and hold. Push both shoulders down and hold. Rotate shoulders to back, to front.
- Squish up face as tight as you can and hold. Stretch face and hold.
- Shake out hands and arms. Shake out legs and feet. Stand up straight.

Vocal Warm Ups

- Pucker and twirl - pucker up your lips and twirl right then left.
- Chew - chew the biggest piece of gum in the world.
- Sputter - sputter lips together like you're a little motorboat.

Tongue Twisters - get your lips and tongue ready to speak, "Red leather, yellow leather" "Rubber baby buggy bumpers"

Vocal vowels - Using vowel change pitch, increase volume, relax mouth

Yawn!! (but not during your speech) it relaxes your vocal cords.

Keep the following tips in mind when it is time to present:

- Warm-up, drink water and mentally rehearse your presentation.
- Find a quiet place to concentrate before the presentation; (restrooms work well).
- Visualize yourself giving your presentation in a calm, organized and engaging manner.
- Stay away from carbonated drinks, coffee, milk, people who may distract you at this point by wanting a long conversation.

Keep in mind that your presentation skills have a great impact on your professional image and the more comfortable, prepared and practiced you are the greater your professional image.

9

Dive in to Success

Dive In

I often find it difficult (as my workshop participants will attest) to stop discussing ways to improve your professional image. I find it very gratifying that even those who are skeptical about the importance of a professional image are converts after the time we've spent together. And that is my hope for you. In addition to knowing *why* it is important to present a professional image, you now have techniques and tools to enhance your current image and improve your visibility, credibility and success at work.

Communicating personal and professional effectiveness is an ongoing process, one certainly worth pursuing. I close my workshops and so this book with the following observation:

Who you are is more important than how you look or what you present

BUT...how you look and what you present can prevent others from getting to know who you are.

I wish you the best in developing your own professional image. A professional image that reflects who you are, how you feel about yourself and the direction you are pursing in your life and career.

About the Author

April Callis is an entertaining and dynamic keynote speaker, seminar leader and consultant. Her combination of practical advice, enthusiasm and cross industry experience make her ideal for senior level groups.

April is President of Springboard Consulting, an organizational development and training firm. As a coach, speaker, and trainer she has written and presented over 1,000 training sessions and seminars for her clients including; The University of Michigan, Ford Motor Company, Foote Health Systems and The State of Michigan. Her courses include:
- Prepare, Practice, Present; Presenting a Professional Image;
- Act Well Your Part - Customer Focused Service;
- Stay in the YES! Pile; Get That Job, and
- Personal Goal Setting for Professional Development.

As a consultant, April focuses on improving performance and provides creative tools to help employees and executives maintain enthusiasm and communication throughout the change process. She has served as a faculty member at Wright College, Triton College, Roosevelt University, and Lansing Community College. April is a frequent guest on local media and hosted an award winning, community issues show on HOM-TV.

She lives in East Lansing, Michigan with her husband Andrew, a Theatre Director and three daughters.

We'd Love to Hear From You!

Email your questions, stories or ideas, which may be incorporated into a future edition of this book.

success@springboard-consult.com

Check out the Springboard web site http://www.springboard-consult.com for articles, tips and inspiration to continue refining your professional image and giving you an even greater bounce on your *Springboard to Success.*